CW00429521

Troubled Times Ahead

Steven Roy Burton

Copyright 2023 Steven Roy Burton

Published in 2023
London, UK

Printed in the UK

The book was published on the behalf of the author, Steven Roy Burton

All rights reserved. No part of this publication may be reproduced, stored in a retrieval system, or transmitted in any means including photocopying, recording or electronic, or mechanical means without prior of the publisher and author.

Jack

Recalculating your moves
On each and every step
With an heart made of stone
You'll never escape

Reinventing the streets
I will pray my victim
Until you are finally free
From this hellish nightmare that you're in

You see my darkened cloak
It's dragging along side the cobbles
And with one step away
I loom in the dark

For now is the time
And for tonight is bitter
But your skin feels like velvet
For my ever-growing desire

Money Is The Root Of All Evil

In a world full of money and greed
When does our voices come out of silence
Because as we stand up and speak
Our young are mistreated by violence

In the playground
Where the young used to play
Now it's a barren land
Where vultures take their prey

Where people seek refuge
So many faces has been seen
But the rest are mistreated
By the everlasting money and greed

Now it's time to change
For the good of ourselves
But money is the root of all evil
And we need to speak the truth

Looking Back

Now I can open my eyes
And say I have survived
The onslaught of this society
Because I have overcome a false reality

Looking back
To what I used to have
I wouldn't turn the clocks
Because the past as made me who I am

With scars to prove it
I look forward to the future
And wherever you are
I know that you will be flying like a shooting star

You are my anchor
And lead me to safety
But I remember
When I was on my knees

You pulled me back
From the brink of death
But if it wasn't for you
I would be dead

Leave It All Behind

From the creation of man
To the bottomless pit of hatred
I give my middle finger
To the extremists

Don't criticise my way of life
I choose who I am
But if you have other ideas
Just leave it all behind

My voice will change this generation
And I hold the light to freedom
I'm gonna speak the truth
Because my words will change a nation

The Fear

Disturbing images fill my mind
A ring of truth
But the chaotic pressure
It's got a hold on my life

Uncertainty
It gets the best of me
And the regrets that are mine
There is no longer a truth left behind

The fear of loving
It's got a hold on my life
And the aftermath
It's like a distant memory of mine

Drowning in a society
Filled with rage and power
But I won't hold you back
Because know that it's all that I have

The Darkness of Man

I can see the darkness
It's following me around
From the bottom of the grave
It will manifest into a deafening sound

The light I hold
It's slowly fading away
From the top of my head
It will be the death of me

Severed by the hands of man
I can feel the presence of the void
It's creeping in
And I can hear the chains rattling

There's no way out
I am trapped in a cage
Trying to find a reason, for this rage
But I can see the darkness, it has consumed me now

Pain

All of her life
This pain inside
She feels alone
All she wants to do, is go back home

All this time
She tries to break the habit
She feels like it's a death grip
All she wants to do, is to wave goodbye

The overdose is too much
Her lifeless body lays
In an effort to love
Her heart is to afraid

Maybe one day
She will find her true love
And he can take this pain
But for now, she's in so much shame

Silenced

The pain that he holds
It quenches her thirst
And as the night unfolds
He is silenced by fear

The blood that falls
It covers the floor
And with a slight twist
He is begging for no more

The horrors that he sees
But for a moment
He closes his eyes
As he becomes her slave

But as the day rises
He watches has she disappears
And in the midst of light
He was silenced by fear

Release Me

Release me from these shackles
And don't let me drown on my own
Cos I can feel the earth pulling me under
But I've tried to fight the battles

The battles that torture me
And it's slipping through my hands
But don't look away
Cos I can see a disfigured reflection looking back

Release me from your system
And don't forget
That I am human
But I can hear the whispers

You throw your hatred
And it's aimed at me
But I don't want to be like you
So I clench my first, and I'm breaking the mirror

Your Shadow

I've lost it all again
And in this life, or another
I'll never grasp the meaning
Because it's the bitter end

Just slow down
I'm losing myself again
But in this life, or another
I'll always be your shadow

Selfish behaviour
Leading to an early grave
Just slow down
Because I'll miss the chance

The chance of life
It's always been you and me
But in a world full of money and greed
I don't stand a chance

Vessels

As the air comes rushing in
And the life force that's at it's tether
I can see the room spinning
But that's not what gives me the shivers

There is an existence
And it's got blackness all around
But I can hear the sirens echoing
As I fall six feet underground

It's got darkness within
This vessel of my body
And with the loneliness
It's a slow reminder of what I used to be

The life that I once had
It will be the warmth of the night
And when the time comes
The end will be in sight

The Prisoner

Mirror mirror on the wall
The person I see
I am not a man
But a painful reminder of what I used to be

Trapped with a monster
And the sentence that has been given
It will be my own nightmare
Because the truth is, redemption is in the air

When the morning comes
I will not fear
But mirror mirror tell me
What is this hell, I cannot share

For this hell, it will be forever
And the person I see, it will always be
Because I have seen my world in decay
But I will not fear the monster I portray

Born Into

I lost a lot of sleep
With a restless mind on repeat
And I'm born into this world
With a cut so deep

I found the answer
To my traumatic disorder
And I'm thrown into the darkness
With my eyes so blind that I cannot see

All the world knows
If I don't repress myself
I'd be better off not knowing
Than to still keep my cut reopening

I'd be better off not knowing
About the future that you hold
But to know is a virtue
And I'm a slave to the world

All the others
They taught me
But now I'm born into a world
Where the world is my enemy

Decorated In Sulphur

Decorated in sulphur
Your devastating words
They still linger
But I won't be afraid

Separate us both
Cos I can feel your scent
And the tree that bares no fruit
It will be the bitter end

Your silence
It means everything
As you walk
I can barely swim

Swim in your devastating words
But I will always be the same
Stuck in the morning dust
Alongside your betrayal

Bloodshed

Bloodshed of your deceit
I'm making way for a change
Because I wanna stop the violence
And the war that you've made

Crippled by this haunted place
You've seen my pain
But whilst I was barely holding on
You took advantage of my shame

You have given me
The bloodshed of your deceit
But I'm traveling down
A black hole made of your deadly ocean

Give back my life
Because I wanna stop
The blood that's been spilled
But you took advantage of my kindness

Another Lie

I'd shed my skin
Just to let you in
Though I may not be the same again
But one more chance, that's what she said

I've given up everything
Though I may not be the person
That you first fell in love with
Just know this…

With my scars showing
I hope that you won't be ashamed
Because with every scar
Comes pain

I'd forget everything for you
Just to let myself know
That you won't run this time
But that was another lie

Here I Am

Here I am once more
Searching for a way out
Wondering if you'd ever notice
Because you're where it all began

I cannot imagine a better day
When the sky opens up and says
Here I am once more
And you gave me the courage to block the pian

And with every second counted
There will be no longer scars to hide
Because when the rattling of cages start
I'll show the world my bleeding heart

Because they know what I've been through
All the sorrow I've felt
And with all the turmoil of the past
Here I am, calling for help

Fragments

These fragments of my death
Somehow, they move into my way
But if I could only hold onto your smile
Than my world would be save

If I only knew what life had to offer
From the light that you hold
I'd be happily ever after
But you went in another direction

These fragments of my life
Somehow, they turn up unexpected
But if only you could see the love I gave
Then, they would be no other

You were the only thing that kept me sane
Even when my days turn colder
It's an instinct from one to another
But you never tried to separate your lies

Hard To Believe

It's sometimes hard to believe
That after all these years
You turned your back
And left me in tears

In this heart of mine
You'll never keep
Because all I have left
Are the long forgotten memories

You choose a life
That played with my mind
You used my good nature
To feed your pride

For all these times
I've done you no wrong
For all the sacrifice
You got up and run

The best part of me
You'll never going to see
Because I will be strong
And I'll p*** you off and move along

I Am More

In a world where there's only the strongest
And as my thoughts were turned away
They'll be time when you'll need me
Because it was you that drove me insane

Because when darkness tries to descends
It's like I'm frozen in time
But I can't hear anything
Only the afterlife that's beckoning

I tried to silence what I cannot see
So I closed my eyes
And I'd prayed for peace
But the terrifying thing is ...

I am more than you expected in life
And I can break through whenever I like
Because it's the strength of the bite
That keeps me known

Demons

From the demons in my mind
To the ever-growing spiral
I'm breaking the silence
And I'm running for the exit

How long before I leave behind the past
The forgotten scars of what used to be
Another night laying in bed
Overthinking possibilities, how to believe

Believe that I'm okay
It's just another faze
But in the bitter end
How long do I have to suffocate in silence

Top-to-toe with the angel of death
I feel the ground trembling
And I can see myself running
From the demons in my mind

Until the Day I Die

Until the day I die
I won't let worry control me
Because nothing else will happen
Until I secure my place in heaven

And this isn't the end of the journey
It might be that you're not here
But all I can think up to now
We all are lost but not forgotten

I've always thought
What is it like to fall asleep under twinkling stars
And what would it feel like
If I showed you my everlasting scars

And as I walk through the night
I know I'll be shown the way
But when the darkness comes in
You'll rescue me just in time

Vicious Cycle

Over and over again
I'll seen the tragic end
Of one's who have called my name
But nothing seems to matter anymore

I'll be searching for the answers
To my scars that will heal in time
And this vicious cycle
Will disconnect me from my life

Because you've seen my weaknesses
And you make me strong through it all
The wilting of days have gone
And now I can hear your call

But for all the lies I created
And as you watch me as I fall
I'll be bleeding out
Because I can't let them break me down

Seeking the Light

This light that I'm seeking
Doesn't reflect my shame
Because the ever-changing world
Won't leave my doubtful mind

Ever since I was born
This shadow keeps following me around
And then I feel a cold breeze
Is this the life that I'm left with

For this is the end
And not for those who've tried
But nothing seems to separate this pain
Because I'm unable to run and hide

With the this darkness looming
Can I ever escape this world
And if it wasn't for you
I'd be a fool throughout my life

Bad Habits Never Die

These thoughts are blurry
And I tried to push away the negativity
Because nobody can understand
All I wanted was these visions to disappear

I'll be watching as the days go by
And my mind will be racing
Because I'll be consumed by a machine
I can't wait to defeat

I'm disabling my nightmares
To let me live my life
But nobody knows what it feels like
To be haunted by the darkness

There were tough times ahead of me
And now as I grow faint
Of these mistakes that lie
Because so many bad habits never die

Valley of Death

When I feel lost and afraid
You've got the right words to say
Even if I feel out of place
You take the dimness of of the day

Your words speak loud
And as I walk through the valley of death
I can feel your warm breath
And it is where I want to be

For this bleeding soul of mine
It will not be able to survive
But when you follow behind
There will be recognition

But as I fall down onto my knees
You bring me back
And whenever you're out of reach
Somehow, you shed light through me

Oxygen

When darkness rolls in
And the light slowly fades
I'll never be tormented
Because you'll give me your oxygen

When silence becomes eternal
And the mountains are too high
I'll never be blinded
Because you're be my guiding light

And when I see the world
I'll never lose my grip
Because the dying of days will soon pass
But I'll put on my armour to fight another day

Raise A Toast

In this haunted ground
That we call our home
It will be the devil's device
That will take over our souls

Lost in a world
Where we try not to sin
But in the bitter end
We rise like a phoenix

And to be more advanced
In a home where dreams are forgotten
We raise a toast
To the brave and the fallen

In this tranquil place
We offer our service
To the ends of the earth
We will see a new form of life

There Is A Subtle Feel

With the withering flows upon the shore
There is tranquil at the porch of my door
As I open up with my thoughts
I am mesmerised by the fond memories

I've opened my mind
And I've let my soul take me
Because there is a subtle feel
To what was my love for the sea

I am free, I muttered
For I have seen the magic flutter
At once was a tragic loss
It's now a happy ever after

I am one with nature
And what I see, is what I believe
But no mortal can resist
The fond memories of the sea

Survived The Game

I can feel myself being exposed
Trying to fight the demon inside
But all I've ever felt is still sinking
And all I ever wanted was to be loved

When my heart wears thin
I thought that I could look to you
But in the end
It's not you that I find comfort in

And with all my scars showing
I thought that you would be there
But where I draw my strength
It's from your bad intentions

It feels like I'm comatose
With every overdose
I try to fight the demons inside
And now I can say I've survived

This Is My Canvas

This is my canvas
And i'm gonna paint you a promise
Where you're with me forever
But until then i'm holding out for your hand

Another day comes and goes
And i feel dead inside
Because this life i hold
It's turning grey and cold

A painted sky full of prayers
Will never be enough
Because this bound i have
Will never bring you back

All these things unsaid
There hanging over me
Like a dancing silhouette
You're never coming back to me

A Changed Man

The scene has changed
And I've been holding my breath
But I can't seem to escape
The best of me is dead

I've been trying to catch myself
As I fall six feet under
But as I find the meaning of my life
It's made me better man inside

It flickers in the dark
The never-ending story unfolds
And I'm a changed man
But only if I let you go of my bitter self

I've been talking to anyone that cares
But sometimes, I stand alone
And now I can smell your perfume scent
Until we meet again, my dearest friend

Angel of Death

From the demons in my mind
To the ever-growing spiral
I'm breaking the silence
And I'm running for the exit

How long before I leave behind the past
The forgotten scars of what used to be
Another night laying in bed
Overthinking possibilities to how to believe

Believe that I'm okay
It's just another faze
But in the bitter end
How long do I have to suffocate in silence

Top-to-toe with the angel of death
I feel the ground trembling
And I can see myself running
From the demons in my mind

Holding On

Carry the weight of the world
And keep me strong through the years
Because of all the love I gave
I'll be forever and always yours

I'm still keep holding on
For another chance
But would you save me
From behind enemy's line

It happens every time
I'm trying to feel alright
But the weight of the world
It's dragging me down

I'm trying to be wholesome
But in the end where I'm holding on
There will be a day when
You'll have to let go off my hand

Wake Up

Do you know how feels
To be locked away from the world
And any chance to hear me call out
Because alone I lie here

With these shackles blocking me to see
And what do you know about how time can heal
When all you do is carry on with your life's
But only if I could watch for a second, her smile

Alone in the dark
Waiting for my freedom
But within your hollow heart
You seem to be the monster I dream about

Have you got the nerve to say anything
With these shackles bounded to me
And you can do your worst
Because nothing what it is, until I wake up

In My Head

With the sun goes down
There's no place I rather be
Because I feel it every time you leave me
I try to get you back and beside me tonight

To be honest
I really hope that someday
We could be together once again
But that was just a fantasy, in my head

The everlasting affair between you and I
It will never end that's what I thought
But when you said those words to me
Never mind, it will probably wait

And as I see you walking away
I want to be honest
I thought we would be soulmates
But it was only in my head

Slight of Hand

In the midst of a masquerade
I can see a soul full of promise
But with a slight hand of change
She's convinced by an innocent kiss

A secret covered in black
A runaway consumed by
What she used to have
But she's only a child

In the history books
A fetish fantasy ascends
And it will blind some folks
But she's groomed by man

In the midst of a revelation
I can feel the soul of one
And with a slight of hand
She is consumed by man

Eye of the Storm

All through my life
I thought I was sentence to prison
But with the brightness of a smile
I am free to roam this barren lands

Through the eye of the storm
I gave everything to erase my doubts
But what kept me from closing in to be banished
It was the way you saw the goodness in me

Edging further away from being mauled
But whilst you patiently waited for me
There'll be better days as we forget how troubles
And when we emerge from the turbulent times

I'm over the moon that I can stand beside you
But in the bitterness of the mind
All I remember is us two
And how we conquer this demon

Printed in Great Britain
by Amazon